BOSTON COMMON PRESS
Brookline, Massachusetts

1998

Boston Common Press
17 Station Street
Brookline, Massachusetts 02146

ISBN 0-936184-27-2
Library of Congress Cataloging-in-Publication Data
The Editors of *Cook's Illustrated*
   How to make cookie jar favorites: An illustrated step-by-step guide to the simplest and best American cookies/The Editors of *Cook's Illustrated*
1st ed.

   Includes 43 recipes and 24 illustrations
   ISBN 0-936184-27-2 (hardback): $14.95
   I. Cooking. I. Title
1998

Manufactured in the United States of America

Distributed by Boston Common Press, 17 Station Street, Brookline, MA 02146.

Cover and text design: Amy Klee
Recipe development: Dawn Yanagihara
Series Editor: Jack Bishop

HOW TO MAKE COOKIE JAR FAVORITES

An illustrated step-by-step guide to the simplest and best American cookies.

THE COOK'S ILLUSTRATED LIBRARY

Illustrations by John Burgoyne

CONTENTS

introduction

I SPEAK FOR THE ENTIRE STAFF OF COOK'S ILLUSTRATED when I say that we are overjoyed to bring you this collection of cookie recipes. Why? For one thing, the recipes are great. And for another, developing these recipes was the most difficult task we've ever undertaken. To find the optimum mix of flour, shortening, sugar, flavorings, and leavener, we had to bake more than 150 separate batches, resulting in over 2,500 cookies! Doesn't sound like hard work? Well, we don't expect sympathy, but another midafternoon cookie taste test is altogether out of the question.

Ultimately, this long and difficult process not only helped us develop the delicious cookie recipes in this book, it also sharpened our understanding of the science of baking. We learned the effects of the protein content of different flours, tasted the difference between butters and other shortenings, discovered when to use baking powder instead of baking soda, found out how to choose between different types of sugar, came to appreciate the effects of cookie size on texture, and learned what to expect from different types of cookie sheets. Cookies are a fascinating microcosm of the world of cooking because little changes in recipes make great differences in finished products.

If you like, of course, you can simply use the recipes here for traditional favorites like Coconut Macaroons, Almond Crescents, or Big and Chewy Oatmeal-Raisin Cookies. You might also be tempted to make a batch of Sugar Cookies with Lime Zest, Chocolate-Peanut Butter Sandwich Cookies, or Marble Icebox Cookies. We also hope that this book will help you learn more about the fundamentals of baking. For all of us, there is a lot to learn.

This book is only one volume in a series that includes *How to Make a Pie*, *How to Make an American Layer Cake*, *How to Stir-Fry*, *How to Make Ice Cream*, *How to Make Pizza*, *How to Make Holiday Desserts*, *How to Make Pasta Sauces*, *How to Make Salad*, and *How to Grill*. Many other titles in this series will soon be available. To order other books, call (800) 611-0759. We also publish *Cook's Illustrated*, a bimonthly publication about American home cooking. For a free trial copy of *Cook's*, call (800) 526-8442.

Christopher Kimball
Publisher and Editor
Cook's Illustrated

chapter one

COOKIE BASICS

HERE ARE THOUSANDS OF COOKIE RECIPES in circulation. Over the years, we have made many of these recipes in our test kitchen and we have come to one startling conclusion. The simplest cookies are usually the best. Chocolate chip, oatmeal, and peanut butter cookies are popular for a reason. They may not be much to look at, but they usually taste better than a fancy cookie that requires a rolling pin, complicated shaping, and icing.

This book explains how to make these classic American cookies, everything from snickerdoodles to molasses-spice cookies. We have tested every variable to come up with recipes that will work every time.

KEY INGREDIENTS

Keep the following items on hand and you will be prepared to make most of the recipes in this book.

BAKING POWDER AND BAKING SODA Cookies are leavened with either baking powder or baking soda. Although cookies do not rise as much as cakes, the leavener does provide some lift and can affect the texture of the cookie.

Baking soda is only fully effective if there is an acid component, such as buttermilk, in the batter for it to react with and create carbon dioxide. In an alkaline (low acid) batter, a teaspoon of baking powder is a more effective leavening agent than an equal amount of soda. Many cookie doughs do not contain acidic ingredients, so baking powder is the most commonly used leavener. Some cookie doughs do contain acidic ingredients, such as brown sugar, molasses, or cocoa, and baking soda may be used in these recipes.

BUTTER We do not recommend using margarine or shortening in most cookie recipes. These fats cannot give cookies the same rich flavor as butter.

We tested eight brands of butter in a variety of recipes to see if the brand or the fat content would make a difference. Higher-fat, European-style butters do make a creamier, richer buttercream frosting, but when making cookies (and most other dishes), we found that freshness is more important than the fat content or a specific brand.

Exposure to light and air will make butter rancid (that's why some sticks are wrapped in foil not paper), as can warm temperatures. The butter compartment on most refrigerator doors tends to be warmer than the rest of the refrigerator and is not the best place to store butter. If you don't use much butter, store it in an airtight plastic bag in the freezer and pull out individual sticks as needed. Butter will maintain peak freshness for several months in the freezer, but no more than two or three weeks in the refrigerator.

One final note about butter. We use unsalted butter when making cookies. We like its sweet, delicate flavor. Peanut butter cookies are the exception to this rule. Salted butter helps bring out the flavor of the peanuts. Otherwise, we prefer the cleaner, fresher flavor of unsalted butter.

⁘ CHOCOLATE CHIPS Most cookie recipes rely on semisweet chips to supply the chocolate flavor. In our testing of major brands, we found that the chips that tasted best straight out of the bag tasted best in cookies. Nestlé, Guittard, Ghirardelli, and Tropical Source (a brand sold in natural food stores) all received high marks.

⁘ COCOA In its natural state, cocoa powder is mildly acidic. Many manufacturers, especially European ones, add an alkaline solution to neutralize the acidity. This processing, called dutching, mellows some of the bitterness and harshness of natural cocoa.

We have found that the choice of natural or dutched cocoa powder often makes a difference in the flavor and appearance of a cookie. In our tests, cookies made with dutched cocoa had a rounder, richer chocolate flavor than those made with natural cocoa. Also, cookies with dutched cocoa were darker and judged more attractive. In a blind tasting of twelve brands of cocoa, we particularly liked dutched cocoas made by Van Leer, Pernigotti, Valrhona, Droste, and Merckens.

EGGS We used large eggs in all the recipes in this book. Cold eggs can cause batters to separate and are harder to mix with other ingredients, so let the eggs sit out on the counter for an hour or two, or warm them in a bowl of hot tap water for five minutes.

FLOUR Cookies are generally made with all-purpose flour. Bread flour is too high in protein and will make cookies dry and tough. Cake flour is too low in protein and will make sandy, crumbly cookies. There are two kinds of all-purpose flour, bleached and unbleached. Bleached flour is treated with chlorine to whiten it and some sources suggest that this process gives the flour a faint off flavor. We wanted to find out, so we tested bleached and unbleached flour in various cookie recipes.

Figure 1.

Sometimes you forget if you have added the salt, leavening, and every spice. Once the flour is in the bowl, add each new dry ingredient in a different spot. If you are interrupted before you are done, simply count the number of ingredients already added.

In a very simple vanilla icebox cookie that does not contain any leavener or other strongly flavored ingredient (such as chocolate, nuts, or peanut butter), we preferred the cleaner flavor of unbleached flour. However, once leavener is added to a recipe, even a simple one such as a sugar cookie, any chemical flavor that the bleached flour might impart to the dough becomes almost impossible to detect. So, with the exception of cookies that do not contain a chemical leavener, use either bleached or unbleached flour as you like.

We measure flour by the dip-and-sweep method. Dip a metal or plastic dry measure into a bag of flour so that the cup is overflowing with flour. Then use a knife or icing spatula to level off the flour, sweeping the excess back into the bag.

⦙⦙ NUTS Many cookies derive crunch and flavor from nuts. We always store nuts in the freezer to prevent them from becoming rancid.

⦙⦙ SALT Although we generally prefer the clean flavor of kosher salt in our savory cooking, we use regular table salt when baking because the smaller crystals are more easily incorporated into a cookie batter.

⦙⦙ SUGAR Granulated sugar is a key ingredient in most cookie recipes. Besides adding sweetness, sugar provides some structure and chew. In fact, very chewy cookies generally have quite a lot of sugar in them.

Many cookie recipes also call for brown sugar, which is granulated sugar with a small percentage of molasses added for flavor and color. (Light brown sugar contains 3.5 percent molasses; dark brown sugar has 6.5 percent molasses.) Brown sugar lends a caramel flavor that is welcome in many cookies. Dark brown sugar has a slightly stronger caramel flavor, but in most cookie recipes the differences are slight. Unless noted, use either variety in the recipes in this book.

When measuring brown sugar, it is important to pack the sugar into the dry measure. We like to use the back of a smaller measure to press brown sugar into the cup (*see* figure 2).

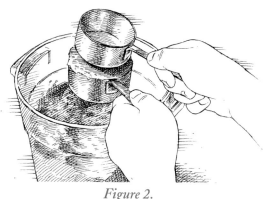

Figure 2.
When a recipe calls for some quantity of packed brown sugar,
fill the correct dry measure with the sugar and use the next
smallest cup to pack it.

Confectioners' sugar is used in cookies where tenderness and a fine crumb are important. Confectioners' sugar is made by pulverizing granulated sugar and combining it with a little cornstarch (about 3 percent of the total weight) to prevent it from clumping together. Because of its fine, powdery consistency, this sugar gives cookies a melt-in-your-mouth texture. Note that small lumps can still form in the box, so we recommend sifting confectioners' sugar before combining it with other ingredients.

⁑ VANILLA EXTRACT When we tested vanilla extracts several years ago, the results were so shocking we repeated the test again and again. It turns out that most people, including

14

pastry chefs, can't tell the difference between a cookie made with vanilla extract and a cookie made with the imitation stuff, which is derived from wood pulp. The differences are apparent in a custard, but in a cookie the quantities are so small and the other ingredients are so flavorful that these differences are hard to detect. But since we are generally loath to recommend ersatz products and since the price differential between the real and the fake is fairly small, we opt for the real thing in this case, too, even if it's hard to taste the difference.

KEY EQUIPMENT

Cookie-making requires very few pieces of equipment. You can even get away with using a wooden spoon instead of an electric mixer, although we do prefer a mixer. The rest of the equipment can be purchased for less than $15, total.

■■ COOKIE SHEETS We tested eleven sheets in a variety of materials and came to some surprising conclusions. First of all, shiny, light-colored sheets do a better job of evenly browning the bottoms of cookies than dark sheets. Most of the dark sheets are nonstick and we found that these pans tend to over-brown cookies. Shiny, silver sheets heat much more evenly, and if sticking is a concern we simply use parchment paper.

In our testing, we also came to prefer sheets with at least one rimless edge. This way we could slide a whole sheet of parchment paper onto a cooling rack without actually touch-

15

ing the hot paper. The open edge also makes it possible to slide cookies on a rack, rather than lifting them onto the rack and possibly dropping them. Our favorite cookie sheet is made by Kaiser out of tinned steel. At just $7, it was also the cheapest sheet we tested.

◗◗ COOLING RACKS These often-neglected items are essential because they allow air to circulate under and around the cookies as they cool. Cookies cooled on a closed sheet might stick or become soggy. Choose a cooling rack that is large and sturdy. Some models have thin wires running in a single direction, but we prefer racks with crosswoven pieces of metal that form a fairly tight grid. These racks, sometimes called icing racks, are usually fairly sturdy. Also, the holes in the grid are very small, making it impossible for cookies to slide through onto the counter, something that often occurs on racks with wires that run in just one direction.

◗◗ MIXER There are two basic types of mixers. Handheld mixers lack the power to knead bread (you need a standing mixer for that) but are fine for cookie doughs.

When shopping for a handheld mixer, look for models that have thin, curved wire beaters rather than the old-fashioned kind with thick posts down the center. This new design does a better job of driving food down into the bowl, improving the efficiency of the mixer while reducing splattering. Wire beaters are also much less likely to become clogged when mixing stiff cookie doughs.

In our testing, we also found that handles that slant up to the front fit the hand better and reduce arm stress more than handles that are parallel to the mixer. We tested nine mixers and found the KitchenAid to be the best choice.

Although standing mixers are not essential for making cookie doughs, they work well and free the cook to gather ingredients or grease a cookie sheet. When selecting a standing mixer, choose one with a single wide, flat beater rather than the two metal beaters commonly found on handheld mixers. The Rival Select and KitchenAid standing mixers have these flat beaters, which operate by planetary action. These beaters are designed to reach the sides and bottom of the bowl to gather up and combine ingredients.

■■ PARCHMENT PAPER When sticking is a potential problem, we recommend lining cookie sheets with parchment paper. The paper also keeps the bottom of the cookies from overbrowning. When the cookies are baked, we usually slide the whole sheet of parchment, with the cookies still attached, right onto the cooling rack. When cooled, the cookies can be peeled away from the paper.

Even when sticking is not an issue, we still use parchment paper. It makes cleanup a snap, and we can reuse cookie sheets for subsequent batches without having to wash them first. When parchment is essential, the recipe directions call for it. Otherwise, use parchment at your discretion.

MIXING COOKIE DOUGH

Most cookie doughs are prepared in the same fashion. The butter is creamed with the sugar until light and creamy. The eggs and other liquids (vanilla or other extracts) are added. Finally, the flour and other dry ingredients, which have been sifted or stirred together, are added.

This process sounds easy (and it is), but there is some important science here. The butter must be properly creamed in order to incorporate the right amount of air into the fat. In our tests, we've consistently found that cookies made with creamed butter are higher and have a lighter texture than those made with butter that is not creamed. We also found that creaming the butter with sugar adds more air than beating the butter alone. That's because the sharp edges of the sugar crystals physically aerate the butter by cutting small air pockets in the fat.

Cookies made with cold butter are often flat because the creaming process was not able to whip enough air into the butter. Ideally, an hour or two before you want to make cookies, remove the butter from the refrigerator and let it warm to about 65 degrees. Butter starts to melt at 68 degrees, so the stick should still be a bit firm when pressed.

If you have forgotten to soften the butter, don't use the microwave to bring it up to room temperature. The microwave will melt the butter in places. Instead, cut the butter into very small bits so they will warm up quickly (*see* figure 3). By the time you have preheated the oven and assembled and measured the remaining ingredients, the butter should be close to 65 degrees.

Butter and sugar can be creamed by hand, but an electric mixer (either handheld or standing) is quicker and more efficient. Most cooks don't cream the butter and sugar long enough and don't get as much volume as they should. The

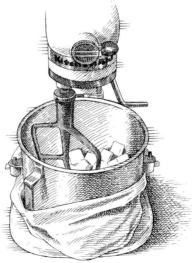

Figure 3.

If you have forgotten to take the butter out of the refrigerator in advance, try cutting the stick into small pieces and placing the pieces in a mixing bowl. You can speed up the warming process by wrapping a towel that has been run under hot tap water around the bowl.

beating times for recipes in this book are for an electric mixer. If you beat the butter and sugar with a wooden spoon, the times will be several minutes longer, depending on your hand strength and speed. When the butter and sugar have lightened in color and become fluffy, you can stop.

Once the butter and sugar are creamed, most recipes call for the addition of eggs and vanilla or other liquids. Make sure the eggs are at room temperature so they don't cause the batter to curdle. At this point, the dry ingredients can be stirred into the batter. You can use an electric mixer—just make sure the speed is set to low.

In many old-fashioned recipes, the flour, leavener, and salt are sifted together before being added to the batter. This was necessary when flour was often lumpy straight from the bag. However, modern flour is presifted and we find this step unnecessary for making cookies. We simply whisk the dry ingredients together in a bowl to make sure that the leavener and salt are evenly distributed in the batter.

The final step in the dough-making process is to add solid ingredients, like chocolate chips and nuts. These should be stirred in by hand since a mixer might break them apart.

SHAPING COOKIES

There are several ways to manipulate a finished dough in order to change the appearance or texture of the baked cookies. In order to inhibit spreading in the oven (and thus prevent the cookies from becoming too thin), chill the dough in the refrigerator for at least one hour.

How the dough is shaped into small pieces will also affect the appearance of the cookies. The cookies in this book all rely on simple shaping methods. (Cookies that require a rolling pin and cutter are not considered.) The doughs in this book are handled in one of three ways.

⠃ DROPPED This is the quickest way to get the dough into the oven. The dough is dropped from a spoon directly onto a cookie sheet. Because the pieces of dough are not round, they spread unevenly in the oven. The result is cookies with thin, crisp edges and thicker centers.

⠃ MOLDED For molded or shaped cookies, each piece of dough is rolled into a ball or otherwise manipulated by hand before being placed on a cookie sheet. When rolled into a ball, the dough is often rolled in sugar before being baked. Shaping the dough into a ball promotes even spreading and thickness in the baked cookies.

⠃ ROLLED AND SLICED The dough is rolled into a log using a piece of plastic wrap, refrigerated until firm, and then sliced into thin rounds and placed on a cookie sheet. These cookies are called icebox, refrigerator, or slice-and-bake cookies. Sandwich cookies are made from thinly sliced

cookies that are cooled and then filled with jam or chocolate and sandwiched together.

BAKING TIPS

To make sure that all the cookies on the baking sheet are
done at the same time, follow these general rules:

∷ **Always preheat the oven.**

∷ **Measure the batter** so that cookies will all be the same size.

∷ **Make sure to leave enough room** between pieces of
dough for cookies to spread in the oven. Two inches is usually a safe distance.

∷ **Halfway through the baking time** reverse the top and
bottom sheets and also rotate each sheet from back to front.

∷ **Watch the clock and check the cookies** a few minutes
before the recipe indicates they will be done. Ovens vary (you
should check yours with an oven thermometer) and cookies
will go from underbaked to overbaked in a very few minutes.

∷ **Consider underbaking the cookies a bit**, especially if you
like them soft and chewy. Allow them to firm up on the sheets
for several minutes before transferring them to a cooling rack.

∷ **When making second and third batches,** do not place
dough directly onto hot cookie sheets. This causes excess

spreading and uneven baking because it will probably take you a few minutes to get all the dough on the sheet. You may arrange pieces of dough on parchment, slide the parchment onto a hot cookie sheet, and then place the cookie sheet immediately in the oven. The hot cookie sheet isn't a problem as long as all the pieces of dough get onto the sheet at the same time and the sheet is immediately put in the oven.

STORING COOKIES

If you want to keep cookies for several days, we suggest storing them in a metal tin at room temperature. You can restore just-baked freshness to chewy cookies by wrapping a single cookie in a sheet of paper towel and microwaving it until soft, 15 to 25 seconds. Cool microwaved cookies before serving. This technique works best with oversized cookies like peanut butter and oatmeal that should be chewy and a bit soft. Do not try this with cookies that should be crisp.

If you know you can't finish off a batch of cookies in a few days, consider freezing part of the dough. Almost every dough can be frozen either in individual portions or as a block. If you have frozen the dough in balls, simply transfer them to a cookie sheet and bake as directed, extending the time in the oven by a few minutes. If the dough is a solid mass, let it thaw in the refrigerator before shaping and baking it.

chapter two

≩

CHOCOLATE
CHIP COOKIES

HOCOLATE CHIP COOKIES COME IN VARIOUS styles, with significant differences in texture, size, and flavor. The dough is a basic sugar cookie, in which some of the granulated sugar has been replaced by brown sugar, which gives them a caramel flavor. Of course, the dough is also studded with chocolate chips and, often, nuts.

Traditional recipes follow the Tollhouse cookie model, made famous on packages of Nestlé chocolate chips. This recipe dates back to the 1930s when Ruth Wakefield, owner of the Toll House Inn in Whitman, Massachusetts, cut up a chocolate bar and added the pieces to a cookie dough. She eventually sold the recipe to Nestlé, which introduced the chocolate morsel in 1939.

These cookies are on the small side (about 2 inches in diameter). The edges are thin, crisp, and golden brown. The center of the cookie is thicker and will bend when the cookies are warm but hardens as the cookies cool and snaps after several hours. The center of this cookie is often cakey, but should not be dry.

The original recipe calls for equal parts of brown and granulated sugar. We found that we like the caramel flavor that the brown sugar gives this cookie and have increased the ratio of brown to granulated sugar to two to one. Modern Tollhouse recipes often omit the water that was part of the original. We found that the water makes the cookies a bit moister and should be added.

An attractive variation on the traditional chocolate chip cookie is the oversized cookie that in recent years bake shops and cookie stores have made their reputation (and a lot of money) by selling. Unlike the traditional recipe made at home, these cookies are thick right from the edge to the center. They are also chewy, even a bit soft. Although we knew at the outset that molding the dough rather than dropping it into uneven blobs would be essential to achieving an even thickness, we didn't realize how challenging making them really chewy would be.

We added more flour or ground oats (as some recipes suggest), which helped the cookies hold their shape and remain thick, but made the texture cakey and dry rather than chewy. When we tried liquid sweeteners, such as molasses and corn syrup, the dough spread too much in the oven and the cookies baked up thin.

At this point in our testing, we decided to experiment with the butter. Some chewy cookies start with melted rather than creamed butter. In its solid state, butter is an emulsion of butter and water. When butter is melted, the fat and water molecules separate. When melted butter is added to a dough, the proteins in the flour immediately grab onto the freed water molecules to form elastic sheets of gluten. The gluten makes a cookie chewy.

Our first attempt with melted butter was disappointing. The dough was very soft from all the liquid, and the cookies baked up greasy. Because the dough was having a hard time absorbing the liquid fat, we reduced the amount of butter from sixteen to twelve tablespoons. We also reduced the number of eggs from two to one to make the dough stiffer.

The cookies were chewy at this point, but they became somewhat tough as they cooled, and after a few hours they were hard. Fat acts as a tenderizer and by reducing the amount of butter in the recipe we had limited its ability to keep the cookies soft. The only other source of fat is the egg. Since our dough was already soft enough and probably could not stand the addition of too much more liquid, we decided to add another yolk (which contains all the fat) and leave out the white. The dough was still stiff enough to shape. When baked, the cookies were thick and chewy and they remained that way when they cooled. Finally, we had the perfect recipe.

Traditional Chocolate Chip Cookies

➤ **NOTE:** *This is our take on the classic Tollhouse cookie, thin and crisp around the edges, thicker and a bit cakier in the middle. The dough can be baked on ungreased sheets, but lining the sheets with parchment will make cleanup easier. When the cookies come out of the oven, they are very soft. Let them cool on the sheets for a minute or two before transferring them to a rack. Makes about 60 cookies.*

2¼	cups all-purpose flour
1	teaspoon baking soda
1	teaspoon salt
½	pound (2 sticks) unsalted butter, softened but still firm
1	cup packed light or dark brown sugar
½	cup granulated sugar
2	large eggs
1	teaspoon vanilla extract
½	teaspoon water
2	cups semisweet chocolate chips
1	cup coarsely chopped walnuts or pecans

INSTRUCTIONS:

1. Adjust oven racks to upper- and lower-middle positions. Heat oven to 375 degrees. Whisk flour, baking soda, and salt together in medium bowl; set aside.

2. Either by hand or with electric mixer, cream together butter and sugars until light and fluffy, about 3 minutes with mixer set at medium speed. Scrape sides of bowl with rubber spatula. Add eggs, vanilla, and water. Beat until combined, about 40 seconds. Scrape sides of bowl.

3. Add dry ingredients and beat at low speed until just combined, 15 to 20 seconds. Add chocolate chips and nuts and stir until combined.

4. Drop batter by tablespoons onto ungreased cookie sheets, spacing pieces of dough about 1 inch apart. Bake, reversing position of cookie sheets halfway through baking, until cookies are light golden brown and outer edges begin to crisp, 8 to 10 minutes. Cool cookies on sheets for 1 to 2 minutes before transferring to cooling racks with wide spatula.

VARIATION:

Cocoa Chocolate Chip Cookies

We like these chocolaty cookies with extra nuts. They won't spread as much in the oven so drop the batter by generous tablespoons onto the baking sheet. We tried both dutched and natural cocoa in this recipe. We thought the dutched cocoa gave the cookies a slightly stronger chocolate flavor, but both types of cocoa worked fine.

Decrease flour to 2 cups and sift ½ cup cocoa powder with other dry ingredients. Increase nuts to 1½ cups. Drop batter by generous tablespoons on cookie sheets and bake 10 to 12 minutes.

29

Thick and Chewy
Chocolate Chip Cookies

➤ **NOTE**: *These oversized cookies are chewy and thick, like many of the chocolate chip cookies sold in gourmet shops and cookie stores. They rely on melted butter and an extra yolk to keep their texture soft. These cookies are best served warm from the oven but will retain their texture even when cooled. To ensure the proper texture, cool the cookies on the cookie sheet. Makes about 18 large cookies.*

2	cups plus 2 tablespoons all-purpose flour
½	teaspoon baking soda
½	teaspoon salt
12	tablespoons (1½ sticks) unsalted butter, melted and cooled until warm
1	cup packed light or dark brown sugar
½	cup granulated sugar
1	large egg plus 1 egg yolk
2	teaspoons vanilla extract
1-1½	cups semisweet chocolate chips

INSTRUCTIONS:

1. Adjust oven racks to upper- and lower-middle positions. Heat oven to 325 degrees. Line two large cookie sheets with parchment paper.

2. Whisk flour, baking soda, and salt together in medium bowl; set aside.

3. Either by hand or with electric mixer, mix butter and sugars until thoroughly blended. Beat in egg, yolk, and vanilla until combined. Add dry ingredients and beat at low speed just until combined. Stir in chips to taste.

4. Roll scant ¼ cup dough into ball (*see* figure 4, page 32). Holding dough ball in fingertips of both hands, pull into two equal halves (*see* figure 5, page 32). Rotate halves ninety degrees (*see* figure 6, page 33) and, with jagged surfaces facing up, join halves together at their base, again forming a single ball, being careful not to smooth dough's uneven surface (*see* figure 7, page 33). Place formed dough onto cookie sheet, leaving 2½ inches between each ball.

5. Bake, reversing position of cookie sheets halfway through baking, until cookies are light golden brown and outer edges start to harden yet centers are still soft and puffy, 15 to 18 minutes. Cool cookies on sheets. When cooled, peel cookies from parchment.

▟ VARIATIONS:

Chocolate Chip Cookies with Coconut and Toasted Almonds

Add 1½ cups sweetened dried coconut and 1 cup toasted sliced almonds along with chips.

Black and White Chocolate Chip Cookies

Substitute ½ cup white chocolate chips for ½ cup of semisweet chips. Add 1 cup chopped pecans with chips.

3 1

Figure 4.
Creating a jagged surface on the top of each dough ball will give
the finished cookies an attractive and somewhat rough appearance.
Start by rolling a scant ¼ cup of dough into a smooth ball.

Figure 5.
Holding the dough ball in the fingertips of both hands, pull the
dough apart into two equal halves.

Figure 6.
Each half will have a jagged surface where it was ripped from the other. Rotate each piece 90 degrees so that the jagged surface faces up.

Figure 7.
Jam the halves back together into one ball so that the top surface remains jagged.

chapter three

≋

CHOCOLATE COOKIES

W E HAVE EATEN ALL KINDS OF CHOCOLATE cookies. Many recipes are similar to the dough used to make traditional Tollhouse cookies, except that some of the flour is replaced by cocoa powder. For our chocolate cookie recipe, we wanted something completely different. The cookie had to be packed with chocolate flavor, both from the dough and from chips. We also wanted the texture to be soft and creamy. We really wanted these cookies to taste like a chocolate bar or truffle baked into the shape of a cookie.

Clearly, we would need to use melted chocolate for both flavor and smoothness. We experimented with semisweet and unsweetened chocolate. Semisweet chocolate was preferable, giving the cookies a better chocolate flavor and a smoother texture. Since we were adding chips to the dough, we tried melted chips instead of melted semisweet chocolate and liked the results just as well.

We encountered a recurring problem in our testing. We wanted to add a lot of chocolate, but the dough was very soft, making it hard to drop and causing the cookies to spread too much in the oven. We also discovered that this batter needed a lot eggs (we settled on three) to give the cookies the smooth, truffle-like consistency we wanted. However, adding so many eggs made the dough even softer.

Many chocolate cookie recipes suggest chilling the dough in the refrigerator to firm up its texture. We found that our dough required two hours to achieve a firm texture. We also discovered that the dough will bake up fine if refrigerated overnight.

Our recipe was almost perfect but needed some final refinements. We added some cocoa powder and liked the results. The cocoa adds an intense, slightly bitter chocolate flavor that balances the sweetness of the chocolate. We found that dutched cocoa tastes richer in this recipe than natural cocoa and makes the cookie darker. The vanilla extract enhances the chocolate flavor and we settled on using a full two teaspoons in our recipe. Although most recipes call for granulated sugar, we added some brown sugar and liked the rich, slightly caramel flavor it imparted.

Chocolate Cookies

➤ **N O T E :** *The batter is fairly thin and needs refrigeration to firm it up and prevent too much spreading in the oven. Even after chilling the batter, these cookies bake up rather flat, but they stay chewy and fudgy after they have cooled. Be careful not to overbake them as the color does not serve as an indicator. Makes about 40 cookies.*

16	**ounces semisweet chocolate chips**
8	**tablespoons (1 stick) unsalted butter**
½	**cup all-purpose flour**
¼	**cup Dutch-processed cocoa powder**
1	**teaspoon baking powder**
¼	**teaspoon salt**
3	**large eggs**
⅔	**cup granulated sugar**
⅓	**cup packed light or dark brown sugar**
2	**teaspoons vanilla extract**

I N S T R U C T I O N S :

1. Melt 8 ounces chocolate chips with butter in double boiler until smooth. Set aside to cool.

2. Sift together flour, cocoa powder, baking powder, and salt. Set aside.

3. Either by hand or with electric mixer, beat eggs with sugars until combined, about 1 minute. Stir in vanilla extract. Add melted chocolate and butter to egg mixture and mix until well combined, about 1 minute. Scrape bottom and sides of bowl. Add dry ingredients and stir until just combined, about 20 seconds. Stir in remaining 8 ounces chocolate chips. Cover bowl with plastic wrap and refrigerate until batter firms, at least 2 hours. (Batter can be refrigerated for one day.)

4. Adjust oven racks to upper- and lower-middle positions. Heat oven to 350 degrees.

5. Drop batter by tablespoons onto parchment-lined cookie sheets, spacing pieces of dough 1½ to 2 inches apart. Bake, reversing position of cookie sheets halfway through baking time, until edges of cookies are just beginning to set and centers are still soft and puffy, 11 to 12 minutes. Slide parchment paper with cookies onto cooling rack. When cooled, peel cookies from parchment.

▓ VARIATIONS:

Chocolate Cookies with White Chocolate Chips and Macadamia Nuts

Substitute 8 ounces white chocolate chips for 8 ounces of semisweet chocolate chips. Stir into finished batter along with 1 cup chopped salted macadamia nuts.

Chocolate Cookies with Orange Zest

Add 1 tablespoon grated orange zest to finished batter along with chocolate chips.

chapter four

3

SUGAR COOKIES

UGAR COOKIES ARE THE SIMPLEST COOKIE YOU can make. Although the ingredient list is short (butter, flour, sugar, eggs, vanilla, leavener, and salt), this cookie can be especially delicious when made right. However, sugar cookies can also be bland and boring. There are no chips or nuts to offer distractions, so the dough itself must be delicious. Our ideal sugar cookie is sweet and buttery, with a soft, chewy texture.

We started testing by focusing on the type and amount of sugar. Some recipes call for confectioners' sugar, but we found that these cookies were too crumbly and not chewy at all. We tried adding some brown sugar, but the caramel

38

flavor felt like a variation to us. It did not deliver the clean, sweet, buttery flavor we wanted for a master recipe. Granulated sugar (and a lot of it) proved to be the best sweetener for flavor and texture.

We next focused on the flour. After several tests we settled on a ratio of one cup butter to two cups flour. This cookie has slightly less flour than many others to allow the buttery flavor to dominate. Cutting the flour made the dough a tad soft, but we reduced the eggs from two in our working recipe down to one and that solved the problem. Reducing the egg also seemed to bring out the flavor of the butter.

We tried baking powder as well as cream of tartar and baking soda. (There are no acidic ingredients in this cookie, so plain baking soda would not work properly.) We felt that the baking powder gave this cookie the cleanest flavor. Several tasters noted a slightly sour flavor in the cookies made with cream of tartar and baking soda.

Our final tests concerned the vanilla. We tried leaving it out and really noticed the difference in this simple cookie. For the best flavor, we found it necessary to use two teaspoons. With less vanilla, the cookies tasted flat or bland.

Sugar Cookies

➤ NOTE: *This is the simplest cookie imaginable, with the flavors of butter, sugar, and vanilla at the fore. The edges are firm but the center is soft and chewy. Makes about 30 cookies.*

2	cups all-purpose flour
1	teaspoon baking powder
½	teaspoon salt
½	pound (2 sticks) unsalted butter, softened but still firm
1¼	cups granulated sugar
1	large egg
2	teaspoons vanilla extract

▦ INSTRUCTIONS:

1. Adjust oven racks to upper- and lower-middle position. Heat oven to 375 degrees. Whisk together flour, baking powder, and salt in medium bowl; set aside.

2. Either by hand or with electric mixer, cream butter and 1 cup sugar until light and fluffy, about 3 minutes with mixer set at medium speed. Scrape sides of bowl with rubber spatula. Add egg and vanilla extract. Beat until combined, about 30 seconds. Add dry ingredients and beat at low speed until just combined, about 30 seconds.

3. Place remaining ¼ cup sugar in shallow bowl. Working

with 1½ tablespoons of dough each time, roll dough into 1½ inch balls (*see* figure 8, page 42). Roll balls in sugar and place on ungreased cookie sheets, spacing balls 2 to 2½ inches apart.

4. Butter bottom of drinking glass with flat bottom that measures about 2 inches across. Dip bottom of glass in remaining sugar and flatten balls of dough with bottom of glass until ⅜ to ½ inches thick and about ¾ inches in diameter (*see* figure 9, page 43). Dip bottom of glass into sugar every two or three cookies.

5. Bake, reversing position of cookie sheets halfway through baking time, until edges of cookies are pale golden, 10 to 11 minutes. Let cookies cool on cookie sheet 2 to 3 minutes before transferring to cooling rack with wide spatula.

⁞ VARIATIONS:

Sugar Cookies with Ginger

Follow Master Recipe, whisking 1 teaspoon ground ginger with dry ingredients. Stir 1 tablespoon chopped crystallized ginger into finished dough.

Sugar Cookies with Lime Zest

Follow Master Recipe, adding 1 teaspoon grated lime zest along with eggs. Place ¼ cup sugar for coating dough in step 3 in food processor. Add 1 teaspoon grated lime zest and process until sugar becomes green and zest is evenly distributed, about 10 seconds. Roll dough balls in lime sugar, gently shaking off excess.

Figure 8.
Take 1½ tablespoons of dough and roll between palms into a ball that measures about 1½ inches in diameter. Roll the ball of dough in sugar and then place the dough on an ungreased cookie sheet.

Figure 9.
Use a drinking glass with a flat bottom that measures about 2
inches across to flatten the balls of dough right on the cookie sheet.
Butter the bottom of the glass before starting and dip it in sugar
every two or three cookies.

chapter five

SNICKERDOODLES

WITH THEIR CRINKLY TOPS AND LIBERAL dusting of cinnamon sugar, chewy snickerdoodles are a favorite in New England. The name is a corruption of a German word that translates as "crinkly noodles."

Traditionally, a snickerdoodle has a subtle tang or sour undertone that contrasts with the cinnamon sugar coating. Most recipes rely on baking soda and cream of tartar as the leavening agent for two reasons. First, the baking soda provides the characteristic tang. Second, the baking soda and cream of tartar cause the cookie to rise very quickly and then to collapse somewhat. The result is the characteristic crinkly top.

We tested both baking powder and the baking soda-cream of tartar combination. As we expected, the latter combination is essential to this cookie. In order to make the cookies especially tangy, we found it helpful not to add vanilla. The vanilla can take away from the sourness, which is fairly subtle.

We noticed that most of the recipes we tested were not nearly chewy enough. We found that increasing the sugar helped, but we wondered why some traditional snickerdoodle recipes contain vegetable shortening or Crisco. Although we generally don't recommend using shortening in cookies (it does not taste as good as butter), we thought it might be worth trying in this case. Unlike butter, which contains about 18 percent water, shortening is 100 percent fat. The water in butter evaporates in the oven and helps the cookies to spread. Since shortening does not contain water, in theory it should help reduce spread in the oven and keep cookies thick and chewy.

Our tests revealed that this bit of common culinary wisdom is in fact true. However, you don't need to use all or half shortening for the desired effect. When we used one part shortening to one part butter, we felt the flavor of the cookie was lacking. After several attempts, we discovered that just one part shortening for every three parts butter is enough to keep the cookies chewy. At this level, the butter flavor still dominates.

Snickerdoodles

➤ **NOTE :** *These old-fashioned cookies are dusted with cinnamon sugar and have a good contrast between crisp exterior and soft, chewy interior. Makes about 30 cookies.*

2¼	cups all-purpose flour
2	teaspoons cream of tartar
1	teaspoon baking soda
½	teaspoon salt
12	tablespoons (1½ sticks) unsalted butter, softened but still firm
¼	cup vegetable shortening
1½	cups plus 3 tablespoons granulated sugar
2	large eggs
1	tablespoon ground cinnamon

▓ **INSTRUCTIONS :**

1. Adjust oven racks to upper- and lower-middle positions. Heat oven to 400 degrees. Grease or line cookie sheets with parchment paper.

2. Whisk flour, cream of tartar, baking soda, and salt together in medium bowl; set aside.

3. Either by hand or electric mixer, cream butter, shortening, and 1½ cups sugar until combined, 1 to 1½ minutes

4 6

with electric mixer set at medium speed. Scrape down sides of bowl with rubber spatula. Add eggs. Beat until combined, about 30 seconds.

4. Add dry ingredients and beat at low speed until just combined, about 20 seconds.

5. Mix remaining 3 tablespoons sugar with cinnamon in shallow bowl. Working with scant 2 tablespoons of dough each time, roll dough into 1½-inch balls. Roll balls in cinnamon sugar and place on cookie sheet, spacing them 2 to 2½ inches apart.

6. Bake, reversing position in oven halfway through baking time, until edges of cookies are beginning to set and centers are soft and puffy, 9 to 11 minutes. Let cookies cool on cookie sheet 2 to 3 minutes before transferring them to cooling rack with wide spatula.

chapter six

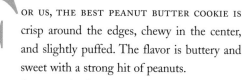

PEANUT BUTTER COOKIES

FOR US, THE BEST PEANUT BUTTER COOKIE IS crisp around the edges, chewy in the center, and slightly puffed. The flavor is buttery and sweet with a strong hit of peanuts.

We started our tests by focusing on the fat. Butter accentuated the peanut flavor, while margarine and Crisco lessened it. The Crisco made the cookie chewier in the center, but we felt the loss in peanut flavor was not worth the added chewiness. We tried peanut oil (thinking this might boost the overall peanut flavor), but the texture was dry and sandy.

From these early tests, we noticed that peanut butter types replicated the results we found with fats. Natural peanut butters with oil on top made the cookies sandy. Commercial brands, which contain partially hydrogenated

48

vegetable oils that are similar to Crisco, made the cookies chewier. We tested both smooth and chunky peanut butter and felt chunky brands contributed more peanut flavor.

We tried using more peanut butter (we even used all peanut butter and no butter), but we still could not get a strong enough peanut flavor. Clearly, we would need peanuts as well as peanut butter. We found that chopped peanuts tend to slip out of the dough. We then ground them in the food processor and worked them directly into the dough, which greatly improved the peanut flavor.

Salt brings out the flavor of peanuts (salted, roasted peanuts taste better than unsalted nuts), and we found that salt also helped bring out the flavor of the peanuts in the cookies. In fact, we found it best to use both salted nuts and salted butter for the strongest peanut flavor.

At this point, we focused our attention on the sweetener. We had been using granulated sugar but wondered if a liquid sweetener might make the cookies chewier. We tried molasses and corn syrup but they could not beat granulated sugar. We tried brown sugar but found the resulting cookies to be too sweet and candyish. However, because the brown sugar did make the cookies taste nuttier, we decided to test half brown sugar and half granulated sugar. This turned out to be ideal, giving the cookies a mild praline flavor that highlighted the flavor of the peanuts.

Peanut Butter Cookies

➤ **NOTE:** *In our testing, we found that salted butter helps bring out the flavor of the nuts. If using unsalted butter, increase the salt to one teaspoon. Makes about 3 dozen cookies.*

2½ cups all-purpose flour

½ teaspoon baking soda

½ teaspoon baking powder

½ teaspoon salt

½ pound (2 sticks) salted butter, softened but still firm

1 cup packed brown sugar

1 cup granulated sugar

1 cup extra-crunchy peanut butter, at room temperature

2 large eggs

2 teaspoons vanilla extract

1 cup roasted salted peanuts, ground in food processor to resemble bread crumbs, about 14 pulses

▦ INSTRUCTIONS:

1. Adjust oven rack to low-center position. Heat oven to 350 degrees. Line large cookie sheet with parchment paper.

2. Whisk flour, baking soda, baking powder, and salt together in medium bowl; set aside.

3. Either by hand or with electric mixer, beat butter until creamy. Add sugars; beat until fluffy, about 3 minutes with electric mixer, stopping to scrape down bowl as necessary. Beat in peanut butter until fully incorporated, then eggs, one at a time, then vanilla. Gently stir dry ingredients into peanut butter mixture. Add ground peanuts; stir gently until just incorporated.

4. Working with generous 2 tablespoons each time, roll dough into 2-inch balls. Place balls on parchment-lined cookie sheet, leaving 2½ inches between each ball. Press each dough ball twice with dinner fork dipped in cold water to make crisscross design (*see* figure 10).

Figure 10.
To make crisscross design, dip a dinner fork in a small bowl of cold water and then press the fork into the dough ball. Rotate the fork 90 degrees and press it into the dough ball a second time.

chapter seven

OATMEAL
COOKIES

WHEN DEVELOPING THIS RECIPE, WE wanted an oversized cookie that was chewy and moist. Most oatmeal cookies seem dry to us, and the flavor of the oats seems too weak. Many recipes don't call for enough oats, and spices often overwhelm the flavor of the oats that are there.

The flavor issues were easily solved. We tested various amounts of oats and found that in order to have a real oat flavor, we needed a ratio of two cups of oats for every cup of flour—far more oats than most recipes use.

To keep the focus on the oats, we decided to eliminate the cinnamon, a common ingredient in most recipes, because it was overpowering the oats. We wanted some spice, however, and chose nutmeg, which has a cleaner, subtler flavor that we liked with oats.

Our cookies tasted good at this point, but we needed to work on the texture. In our tests, we found that a high proportion of butter to flour helped to keep the cookies moist. We settled on two parts butter to three parts flour.

We found that shaping the dough into two-inch balls (rather than dropping the meager rounded tablespoon called for in most recipes) helped keep the cookies moister and chewier, especially in the center, which remains a bit underbaked in an oversized cookie.

Our final tests involved the sugar. We experimented with various amounts and found that adding a full cup each of both brown and granulated sugar delivered the best results, a cookie that was especially moist and rich. Sugar makes baked goods moister and more tender because it helps them hold onto water during the baking process. In addition, sugar encourages exterior browning, which promotes crispness.

Oatmeal Cookies

➤ **NOTE :** *If you prefer a less sweet cookie, you can reduce the white sugar by one-quarter cup, but you will lose some crispness. Do not overbake these cookies. The edges should be brown but the rest of the cookie should be very light in color. Parchment paper makes for easy cookie removal and cleanup, but it is not a necessity. If you don't use parchment, cool the cookies on the baking sheet for two minutes before transferring them to a cooling rack. Makes about 18 large cookies.*

½	pound (2 sticks) unsalted butter, softened but still firm
1	cup packed light brown sugar
1	cup granulated sugar
2	large eggs
1½	cups all-purpose flour
½	teaspoon salt
½	teaspoon baking powder
¼	teaspoon freshly grated nutmeg
3	cups rolled oats
1½	cups raisins (optional)

⠿ INSTRUCTIONS :

1. Adjust oven racks to low and middle positions. Heat oven to 350 degrees. Line two large cookie sheets with parchment paper, if using.

2. Either by hand or with electric mixer, beat butter until creamy. Add sugars; beat until fluffy, about 3 minutes. Beat in eggs one at a time.

3. Whisk flour, salt, baking powder, and nutmeg together in medium bowl. Stir dry ingredients into butter-sugar mixture with wooden spoon or large rubber spatula. Stir in oats and optional raisins.

4. Working with generous 2 tablespoons of dough each time, roll dough into 2-inch balls. Place balls on parchment-lined cookie sheet, leaving at least 2 inches between each ball.

5. Bake until cookie edges turn golden brown, 22 to 25 minutes. (Halfway during baking, turn cookie sheets from front to back and also switch them from top to bottom.) Slide cookies on parchment onto cooling rack. Let cool at least 30 minutes before peeling cookie from parchment.

■■ VARIATIONS:

Date Oatmeal Cookies

Follow Master Recipe, substituting 1½ cups chopped dates (*see* figure 11, page 57) for raisins.

Ginger Oatmeal Cookies

Follow Master Recipe, adding ¾ teaspoon ground ginger to flour and other dry ingredients and omitting raisins.

Chocolate Chip Oatmeal Cookies

Follow Master Recipe, omitting nutmeg and substituting 1½ cups semisweet chocolate chips for raisins.

Nut Oatmeal Cookies

Follow Master Recipe, decreasing flour to 1⅓ cups and adding ¼ cup ground almonds and 1 cup chopped walnut pieces along with oats. (Almonds can be ground in food processor or blender.) Omit raisins.

Orange and Almond Oatmeal Cookies

Follow Master Recipe, omitting raisins and adding 2 tablespoons minced orange zest and 1 cup toasted chopped almonds (toast nuts in 350-degree oven for 5 minutes) along with oats.

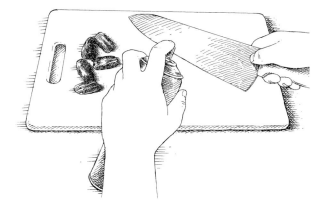

Figure 11.
Dried fruit, especially dates, very often sticks to the knife when you try to chop it. To avoid this problem, coat the blade with a thin film of vegetable oil spray just before you begin chopping any dried fruit. The chopped fruit doesn't cling to the blade and the knife stays relatively clean.

chapter eight

⅗

MOLASSES-SPICE COOKIES

MANY MOLASSES-SPICE COOKIES ARE REAL-ly gingersnaps. They are hard and dry and not nearly sweet enough. We wanted to create an oversized cookie that was especially soft and chewy. We also wanted the cookie to have a strong molasses flavor with a good hit of sweetness. We started by testing the sweetener since we figured that the molasses would be the key to the puzzle.

We quickly found that too much molasses will impart a bitter quality to the cookies. Cookies made with a lot of molasses may be soft and chewy, but they won't taste very good. We tried cutting back on the amount of molasses but

58

the cookies were too bland. Brown sugar, which is made with a small amount of molasses, proved to be the answer. Unlike straight molasses, brown sugar has no harsh flavors. After several tests, we settled on the following formula as the ideal compromise between sweetness and good molasses flavor—one half cup each of dark brown sugar and granulated sugar along with one third cup of molasses.

We found that using a fair amount of sweetener helped make the cookies soft and chewy. The other trick was to underbake the cookies a bit. Even with all this sweetener, these cookies can become hard if overbaked. Since the color of the cookies is so dark, err on the side of underbaking.

Molasses-spice cookies need to have a good spice flavor as well. Cinnamon, ginger, cloves, and allspice are the usual choices in most recipes. We especially like the flavor of the cinnamon and ginger in these cookies. The cloves are good, but they can dominate if used too freely. We settled on ¾ teaspoon as the right amount. Allspice is more problematic. In small amounts, this spice can sharpen the molasses flavor without seeming obtrusive, but we found that adding more than ¼ teaspoon made the cookies harsh and even bitter.

Molasses-Spice Cookies

➤ NOTE: *These oversized cookies are especially attractive, with a rich, dark color, almost perfectly round edges, a surface marked with deep cracks, and an even thickness from the edge to the center. They stay incredibly soft and chewy, even days after they are baked. It is important to underbake the cookies (they won't look done when you take them out of the oven) and then let them firm up as they cool on the baking sheet. If you overbake these cookies, they will become dry and crisp. Makes about 20 large cookies.*

2 ¼   cups all-purpose flour

2   teaspoons baking soda

½   teaspoon salt

1½   teaspoons ground cinnamon

1   teaspoon ground ginger

¾   teaspoon ground cloves

¼   teaspoon ground allspice

12   tablespoons (1½ sticks) unsalted butter, softened but still firm

½   cup packed dark brown sugar

½   cup plus ⅓ cup granulated sugar

1   large egg

1   teaspoon vanilla extract

⅓   cup unsulphured molasses

▦ **INSTRUCTIONS:**

1. Adjust racks to upper- and lower-middle positions. Heat oven to 375 degrees. Whisk flour, baking soda, salt, and spices together in medium bowl; set aside.

2. Either by hand or with electric mixer, cream butter, brown sugar, and ½ cup granulated sugar until light and fluffy, about 3 minutes with mixer set at medium speed. Scrape sides of bowl with rubber spatula. Add egg, vanilla extract, and molasses. Beat until combined, about 30 seconds. Scrape sides of bowl.

3. Add dry ingredients and beat at low speed until just combined, about 30 seconds.

4. Place remaining ⅓ cup granulated sugar in shallow bowl. Working with 2 tablespoons of dough each time, roll dough into 1¾-inch balls. Roll balls in sugar and place on ungreased cookie sheets, spacing them 1½ to 2 inches apart.

5. Bake, reversing position of cookie sheets halfway through baking, until outer edges begin to set and centers are soft and puffy, 11 to 13 minutes. Cool cookies on sheets for 2 to 3 minutes before transferring to cooling racks with wide spatula.

▞ **VARIATIONS:**

Molasses-Spice Cookies with Orange Zest

These cookies have orange zest in the dough as well as in the sugar coating. The zest in the sugar coating prevents the sugar from melting completely and clumps up a bit. The result is a frosted orange appearance that is quite attractive.

Follow Master Recipe, stirring 2 teaspoons grated orange zest into dough after dry ingredients have been incorporated. Place ⅓ cup sugar for coating dough in step 4 in food processor. Add 1 teaspoon grated orange zest and process until sugar becomes yellow and zest is evenly distributed, about 10 seconds. Roll dough balls in orange sugar, gently shaking off excess.

Glazed Molasses-Spice Cookies

Follow Master Recipe, preparing and baking cookies as directed. When cookies have cooled, sift 1½ cups confectioners' sugar and then whisk with 2 tablespoons milk until smooth. Dip spoon into glaze and drizzle over cookies (*see* figure 12).

Figure 12.
Using a spoon to drizzle glaze over the cookies is fast and efficient.
Place the cooled cookies back onto a cooled baking sheet.
(Line the cookie sheet with parchment paper to speed clean up,
if you like.) Dip the spoon into the glaze and move the spoon
over the cookies so that the glaze drizzles down onto them.
Dip the spoon into the glaze as needed.

chapter nine

℈

ALMOND CRESCENTS

OOD ALMOND CRESCENTS HAVE A FINE, delicate crumb that is not dry or coarse. They melt in your mouth and seem light and buttery. Of course, they also must have a good nut flavor.

Confectioners' sugar is commonly used to give cookies an especially fine, melting texture. Because this sugar has been pulverized and then cut with cornstarch, it is supposed to make cookies that are tender and light. To test this theory, we made batches of crescents with both granulated and confectioners' sugar. There was no comparison. The cookies with granulated sugar were coarse and crisp. The cookies made with confectioners' sugar were light and delicate with a particularly fine texture.

In order to make the cookies especially light, we found it helpful to use a slightly lower amount of flour than is commonly called for in most almond crescent recipes. In fact, we used only as much flour as was necessary to make a dough that could be easily rolled into short ropes and then shaped into crescents.

We next focused on the nuts. Chopped nuts are too coarse for this dough. We found it necessary to grind the nuts in a food processor. Many recipes that we tried did not have nearly enough nuts. A full 1½ cups is required for good nut flavor. We also found it helpful to add a little almond extract.

Although almonds are the most traditional flavor for crescent cookies, pecans and walnuts are equally appealing.

Almond Crescents

➤ NOTE: *These melt-in-your-mouth cookies get their light, buttery texture from confectioners' sugar, but it's imperative to sift this sugar to remove all lumps. Makes about 4 dozen cookies.*

1 ¾	cups all-purpose flour
¾	teaspoon salt
½	pound (2 sticks) unsalted butter, softened but still firm
1 ¾	cups confectioners' sugar, sifted
1 ½	teaspoons vanilla extract
½	teaspoon almond extract
1½	cups blanched whole almonds, ground in food processor until quite fine

▓ INSTRUCTIONS:

1. Adjust oven racks to upper- and lower-middle positions. Heat oven to 350 degrees. Whisk flour and salt together in medium bowl; set aside.

2. Either by hand or with electric mixer, cream butter and ¾ cup sugar until light and fluffy, about 2 minutes with mixer set at medium speed. Scrape sides of bowl with rubber spatula. Stir in vanilla and almond extracts.

3. Add ground almonds and flour mixture and mix at low speed until just combined, about 40 seconds.

4. Working with 1 tablespoon of dough each time, roll dough into 1¼-inch balls. Roll each ball between hands into rope that measures 3 inches long (*see* figure 13, page 68). Shape ropes into crescents on ungreased cookie sheet (*see* figure 14, page 68), spacing them 1 to 1½ inches apart.

5. Bake, reversing position of cookie sheets halfway through baking, until edges of cookies are golden brown, 15 to 17 minutes. Cool cookies on cookie sheet about 2 minutes before transferring them to cooling rack with wide spatula.

6. When cookies have completely cooled, roll them in remaining 1 cup confectioners' sugar until evenly coated (*see* figure 15, page 69).

▇ VARIATIONS:

Pecan or Walnut Crescents

Follow Master Recipe, substituting 1¾ cups pecans or walnuts for almonds. Omit almond extract.

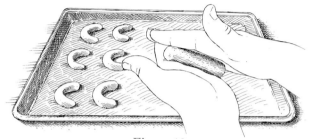

Figure 13.
Working with 1 tablespoon of dough each time, roll dough into
1 ¼-inch balls. Roll each ball between palms into a rope that
measures 3 inches long.

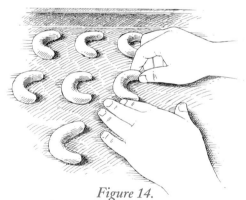

Figure 14.
Place the ropes on an ungreased cookie sheet and turn up the
ends to form a crescent shape.

Figure 15.
Rolling the cooled crescents in a bowl of confectioners' sugar
creates a thicker, more attractive coating than sifting the
sugar over the cookies.

chapter ten

COCONUT MACAROONS

TOO MANY MACAROONS ARE SWEET WITH little real coconut flavor. They also can be dry. We wanted to create a coconut macaroon that was moist without being sticky. We also wanted the macaroon to have a strong coconut flavor with only enough sugar to complement the coconut, not overwhelm it.

There are three styles of coconut macaroons. The simplest recipes combine coconut, egg whites, and sugar. Another recipe style calls for the making of a meringue (the egg whites are beaten with the sugar until stiff) and then

70

the folding in of the coconut. A third style combines the coconut with sweetened condensed milk.

We made all three styles of coconut macaroon and concluded that simpler is better. The macaroons made with a meringue were too light and airy—like a meringue. The macaroons made with the sweetened condensed milk were sticky and much too sweet and dense. The cookies with just coconut, unbeaten egg whites, and sugar had the best texture and flavor, although they needed improvement.

We first focused on increasing the coconut flavor. We quickly discovered that sweetened flaked coconut, the kind sold in supermarkets, is part of the problem. The cookies need a certain amount of sugar to hold together and using sweetened coconut makes it impossible to get the sugar to coconut ratio in balance.

When we switched to grated unsweetened coconut, which is sold in natural food stores and some gourmet shops, the flavor of the cookies improved dramatically. Because this product is grated rather than flaked, the texture of the cookies was also smoother and more appealing.

At this point, our macaroons were still a bit dry. However, we found that a small amount of corn syrup kept them moist and even a bit gooey, but did not make them soggy. However, don't use more than one tablespoon of corn syrup or the cookies will be too wet and sticky.

Coconut Macaroons

➤ **NOTE:** *The great thing about these cookies is that they are not the cloyingly sweet confections that commonly pass as macaroons. In our testing, we found that grated unsweetened coconut (sold in natural food stores and some gourmet shops) is the key to a macaroon that tastes like coconut. Makes about 2 dozen cookies.*

2	large egg whites
1	tablespoon corn syrup
1	teaspoon vanilla extract
½	cup sugar
2 ½	cups grated unsweetened coconut (*see* note above)
¼	teaspoon salt

INSTRUCTIONS:

1. Adjust oven racks to upper- and lower-middle positions. Heat oven to 325 degrees. Line two cookie sheets with parchment paper.

2. By hand, lightly beat egg whites with corn syrup and vanilla extract in small bowl until thoroughly combined. Stir together sugar, coconut, and salt in another bowl. Add egg white mixture to coconut mixture and stir until evenly moistened.

3. Drop 1½ tablespoons of batter onto cookie sheet, spacing them about 1½ inches apart (*see* figure 16, page 74). When cookie sheet is full, dampen fingers with cold water and loosely shape each mound of batter into haystack shape (*see* figure 17, page 75).

4. Bake, reversing position of cookie sheets halfway through baking, until macaroons are golden brown around edges, 8 to 10 minutes. Cool cookies on sheets about 5 minutes before transferring to cooling rack.

⁞ VARIATION:

Coconut Macaroons with Chocolate Chips

Follow Master Recipe, stirring ½ cup semisweet chips into finished batter.

Figure 16.
Use a tablespoon measure to drop mounds of coconut that measure
about 1½ tablespoons each onto a parchment-lined cookie sheet.
Leave about 1½ inches between each mound of coconut.

Figure 17.
Once the cookie sheet is covered with mounds of coconut, moisten
your fingers with cold water and shape each mound into the
characteristic loose haystack or pyramid shape.

chapter eleven

ICEBOX
COOKIES

ICEBOX COOKIES, ALSO CALLED REFRIGERATOR OR
slice-and-bake cookies, are an American invention.
A buttery cookie dough is rolled into a log, chilled
until firm, then sliced and baked. The result is a thin,
flat cookie. If you like moist, chewy cookies, look elsewhere.

When developing our master recipe for icebox cookies,
we had several goals. We wanted these wafer-like cookies to
have a crumbly, sandy texture that was tender, not crisp or
hard. We also wanted the flavor to be as rich and buttery as
possible. Finally, we did not want the dough to be sticky or
temperamental. Chilling will make almost any dough firm
enough to slice. However, the dough for an icebox cookie

must be manipulated right from the mixer. An overly soft or tacky dough would prove problematic.

Our first goal was to make the cookie thin and flat. Some recipes contain baking powder and others do not. We found that cookies made with baking powder were either too soft or too cakey. Since an icebox cookie is by definition thin, we did not want any lift from a leavener and eliminated it from our working recipe.

Although the cookies made without leavener were thin, we found that they often had bubbles in them. We wanted an even crumb that was dense and tender. Something was still causing the cookies to rise. We tried creaming the butter less and found that reducing the beating time from our standard three minutes to just one minute was the trick. Extensive creaming of the butter beats in too much air. The result is tiny air pockets that prevent the cookies from baking up perfectly flat.

We next focused on the sugar. Granulated sugar is used in recipes where sturdiness is a must, like in rolled sugar cookies. However, we wanted cookies that were finer-textured and a bit crumbly. Confectioners' sugar is used in many cookie recipes to lend a melt-in-the-mouth texture, but we found that using all confectioners' sugar made icebox cookies with a texture that was too crumbly. After several tests, we settled on a ratio of three parts granulated sugar to two parts confectioners' sugar.

We also preferred the cleaner flavor of unbleached flour. Bleached flour gave these cookies a slight off flavor. The difference was slight, but noticeable. We wondered why we could not detect any difference in other cookies, even in our simple sugar cookie (*see* chapter 4). Then we realized that the other cookies have more ingredients, including leavener, which obscured the differences in the flours.

Most icebox cookie recipes rely on whole eggs, and in our testing, we found that they were often quite pale and not very attractive. Using two yolks (rather than one whole egg) solved this problem and also added some more fat. The whites make the dough sticky and should be discarded or saved for another recipe.

Finally, we tested various oven temperatures. We found that a low oven temperature of 325 degrees helps the cookies hold their shape in the oven. At the lower temperature they also brown more evenly (at higher temperatures the edges burn before the center cooks through) and the texture is more delicate and fragile.

Vanilla Icebox Cookies

➤ NOTE: *These wafer-like cookies bake up fairly thin with a crumbly, sandy texture. We found that the cleaner flavor of unbleached flour makes a difference in this simple cookie that does not contain any leavener. Makes about 45 cookies.*

2¼	cups all-purpose flour, preferably unbleached
½	teaspoon salt
½	pound (2 sticks) unsalted butter, softened but still firm
¾	cup granulated sugar
½	cup confectioners' sugar, sifted
2	large egg yolks
2	teaspoons vanilla extract

⸬ INSTRUCTIONS:

1. Whisk together flour and salt in medium bowl; set aside.

2. Either by hand or electric mixer, cream butter and sugars until light and fluffy, 1 to 1½ minutes with mixer set at medium speed. Scrape sides of bowl with rubber spatula. Add yolks and vanilla extract and beat until incorporated, 15 to 20 seconds. Scrape bowl with rubber spatula. Add flour mixture and mix at low speed until dough forms and is thoroughly mixed, about 25 to 30 seconds.

3. Dough will be soft but should not be sticky. If sticky, chill for 10 to 15 minutes. Divide dough in half. Working with one half at a time, roll dough on work surface into log measuring about 6-inches long and 2-inches thick (*see* figure 18, page 82). Wrap each log in plastic and refrigerate at least 2 hours or up to 3 days. (Dough can be frozen up to one month. Wrap logs in plastic and then foil before freezing.)

4. Adjust oven racks to upper- and lower- middle positions. Heat oven to 325 degrees. Grease or line cookie sheets with parchment paper.

5. Unwrap dough logs one at a time and with sharp knife, cut dough into ¼-inch-thick slices (*see* figures 19 and 20, page 82). Place slices on cookie sheets, spacing them ½ to 1 inch apart.

6. Bake, reversing positions halfway through baking time, until edges begin to brown, about 14 minutes. Cool cookies on cookie sheets for 2 minutes, then transfer to cooling rack with wide spatula.

▓ VARIATIONS:

Chocolate Icebox Cookies

Follow Master Recipe, reducing flour to 2 cups and whisking flour and salt with ¼ cup sifted dutched-process cocoa. Add 2 ounces melted and cooled semisweet chocolate to batter along with yolks and vanilla.

Marble Icebox Cookies

Follow Master Recipe, making half recipe of both Vanilla

and Chocolate Icebox Cookies. Combine doughs as directed in figures 21 and 22, page 83. Chill, slice, and bake.

Cinnamon-Sugar Icebox Cookies

Save the egg whites when separating the yolks for the dough.

Follow Master Recipe, brushing chilled logs with beaten egg whites. Roll logs in mixture of 3 tablespoons sugar and 2 teaspoons ground cinnamon. Slice and bake as directed.

Ginger Icebox Cookies

Follow Master Recipe, whisking 2 teaspoons ground ginger with flour and salt.

Glazed Lemon Thins

Follow Master Recipe, adding 1 tablespoon grated lemon zest with yolks and vanilla. For glaze, sift 1 cup confectioners' sugar and then whisk with 1 tablespoon heavy cream and 4¼ teaspoons lemon juice until smooth. Drizzle glaze over cooled cookies with spoon (*see* figure 12, page 63).

Butterscotch Icebox Cookies

A maple glaze is especially good with these cookies. Sift 1 cup confectioners' sugar and then whisk with 3 tablespoons maple syrup and 1 tablespoon milk until smooth. See figure 12, page 63 for information on using a spoon to drizzle cooled cookies with glaze.

Follow Master Recipe, replacing granulated sugar with equal amount of brown sugar.

Figure 18.
Pat half of the dough into a rough log shape. Then roll with your hands to make a smooth log about 6-inches long and 2-inches thick. Lift the dough log onto a piece of plastic wrap and roll to seal. Chill dough before baking.

Figure 19.
We find that the chilled dough can soften by the time you cut an entire 6-inch log into slices. Therefore, we recommend slicing the unwrapped log in half and placing one half back in the refrigerator while you slice the other half.

Figure 20.
Using a very sharp chef's knife, slice the log of dough into thin rounds. To prevent one side from flattening, roll the dough an eighth of a turn after every slice.

Figure 21.

To make marble cookies, break the vanilla and chocolate doughs
each into four pieces. Lay the pieces next to each other on a clean
counter, alternating pieces of vanilla and chocolate dough. Press
the pieces together to form a single mass.

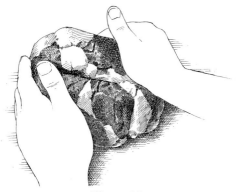

Figure 22.

Lightly knead the dough three or four times so that it becomes
marbled. Do not overwork the dough or you will lose the
marbling effect. Form the dough into logs as directed in
figure 18. Chill, slice, and bake.

83

chapter twelve

SANDIES

ANDIES ARE A TYPE OF ICEBOX OR SLICE-AND-bake cookie that relies on ground nuts to take the place of some flour. Their texture is fine and light, but these cookies are crisp rather than crumbly. In some ways, they are like shortbread cookies packed with nuts.

We found that ground nuts give the dough a rich flavor. However, we found it necessary to add some chopped nuts for texture (it's nice to have a bit of crunch) and appearance.

We experimented with various sweeteners, trying to find one that would highlight the flavor of the nuts. Maple syrup gives the dough a great flavor, but liquid sweeteners (we also tried molasses) make the dough sticky and the cookies bake up heavy and leaden.

We tried using brown sugar and liked the caramel flavor, which works especially well with nuts. Either light or dark brown sugar is fine in this cookie, but dark brown gives better color and a stronger molasses flavor. Again, we liked the effect of a little confectioners' sugar in this dough. It helps give sandies their fine, delicate texture.

We tried adding baking powder (and later baking soda), but we found leaveners make these cookies too cakey. We like sandies that are fairly thick and found that slicing them thick was the best way to get some height in the finished product.

Pecan Sandies

➤ **NOTE:** *Sandies are thicker than your average icebox cookie and have a melt-in-the-mouth texture that comes from ground nuts being added to the dough. Confectioners' sugar also gives these cookies an especially fine, smooth texture. Makes about 2 dozen cookies.*

1½	cups all-purpose flour
½	teaspoon salt
¼	teaspoon ground cinnamon
1	cup plus 2 tablespoons chopped pecans
12	tablespoons (1½ sticks) unsalted butter, softened but still firm
¼	cup confectioners' sugar, sifted
6	tablespoons packed light or dark brown sugar
1	large egg yolk

INSTRUCTIONS:

1. Whisk together flour, salt, and cinnamon in medium bowl. Pulse ½ cup plus 2 tablespoons pecans in food processor until fine. Nuts should be dry and fluffy. (Do not overprocess or nuts will become damp and oily.) Stir ground pecans and remaining ½ cup chopped nuts into flour mixture; set aside.

2. Either by hand or electric mixer, cream together butter and sugars until light and fluffy, about 3 minutes. Beat in yolk until incorporated, about 20 seconds. Add flour mixture and mix on low speed until dough just comes together, 25 to 30 seconds.

3. Roll dough on work surface into log measuring about 8-inches long and 2-inches thick. Wrap log in plastic and refrigerate at least 2 hours or up to 3 days. (Dough can be frozen up to 1 month. Wrap log in plastic and then foil before freezing.)

4. Adjust oven racks to upper- and lower-middle position. Heat oven to 325 degrees. Unwrap dough log and with sharp knife, cut dough into ⅜-inch-thick slices (*see* figures 19 and 20, page 82). Place slices on ungreased cookie sheets, spacing them ½ to 1 inch apart.

5. Bake, reversing positions halfway through baking time, until edges begin to brown, 16 to 18 minutes. Cool cookies on cookie sheets for 2 minutes, then transfer to cooling rack with wide spatula.

VARIATIONS:

Walnut Sandies

Follow Master Recipe, replacing pecans with equal amount of chopped walnuts.

Almond Sandies

Follow Master Recipe, replacing pecans with equal amount of whole blanched almonds that have been toasted in 350-degree oven for 8 minutes, cooled, and then chopped. Add ¼ teaspoon almond extract with egg yolk.

chapter thirteen

SANDWICH COOKIES

ANDWICH COOKIES LOOK IMPRESSIVE BUT ARE actually very simple to make. Two thin, crisp cookies are sandwiched together with a little filling. Sandwich cookies are made from an icebox cookie dough that is sliced very thin. We found it necessary to reduce the baking time for these thinner cookies, but otherwise the cookie part of the recipe is the same.

We tested three chocolate fillings. Plain melted chocolate was too runny to use. A chocolate buttercream frosting, made with butter, milk, and confectioners' sugar, was too creamy and soft. A ganache, which is made by stirring chopped chocolate into hot cream, is much simpler to prepare than buttercream and holds its shape better. It also has a very strong chocolate flavor. The ganache will firm up as it cools, so wait until it reaches room temperature before using it to make the sandwich cookies.

Jam is another common filling for sandwich cookies. We found it imperative to use jam that does not have any big chunks of fruit, which will keep the two cookies from coming together properly to form a sandwich. If necessary, you can strain the jam through a mesh sieve to remove pieces of fruit.

Be stingy with the filling. You don't want the filling to ooze out. Also, we found that it is not possible to fill the cookies very far in advance. The filling will make the cookies soggy rather quickly. At most, filled sandwich cookies can be stored for two hours. If you like, you can bake the cookies and keep them in an airtight container for two days before adding the filling.

Chocolate Sandwich Cookies

➤ NOTE: *The ganache filling has a good chocolate flavor and will hold its shape once cooled to room temperature. Makes about 30 sandwich cookies.*

1	recipe Chocolate Icebox Cookies (page 80)
½	cup heavy cream
12	ounces bittersweet or semisweet chocolate, chopped

▓ INSTRUCTIONS:

1. Prepare dough for chocolate icebox cookies as directed. Cut cookies into ⅛-inch-thick rounds and reduce baking time by a minute or two. Cool cookies completely. (Cookies can be stored in an airtight container for up to 2 days.)

2. Place cream in small saucepan and bring to simmer. Turn off heat and add chocolate. Wait 3 minutes, then whisk until smooth. Let mixture cool to room temperature, at least 30 minutes.

3. Following figures 23 and 24 on page 92, fill cookies with chocolate mixture. Serve within 2 hours.

∷ VARIATIONS:

Mint Chocolate Sandwich Cookies

Follow recipe for Chocolate Sandwich Cookies, adding 1 teaspoon mint extract to cooled chocolate filling.

"Oreo" Cookies

The chocolate cookies and white filling may look like an Oreo, but the flavor is far superior. The filling relies on melted white chocolate mixed with sour cream to cut some of the cloying sweetness of the chocolate.

Follow recipe for Chocolate Sandwich Cookies, omitting cream and replacing bittersweet or semisweet chocolate with an equal amount of white chocolate. Melt white chocolate in double boiler. Stir in ½ cup sour cream and cool to room temperature, about 15 minutes. Use filling as directed.

Chocolate-Peanut Butter Sandwich Cookies

Follow recipe for Chocolate Sandwich Cookies, replacing chocolate filling with 1 cup smooth peanut butter beaten with 4 tablespoons softened butter and 1 cup confectioners' sugar, sifted, until fluffy.

Figure 23.
Place half of the baked cookies on a cool cookie sheet, with the flat
undersides facing up. Place a small mound of filling in the center
of each cookie.

Figure 24.
Take a plain baked cookie and attach the flat underside to one of
the cookies that has been dolloped with a mound of filling. Press
gently to spread the filling between the two cookies.

Linzer Cookies

➤ **NOTE:** *Almond cookies filled with raspberry jam are a classic. However, feel free to create your own combinations using the pecan or walnut sandies and other kinds of jam. Makes about 20 sandwich cookies.*

1 recipe Almond Sandies (page 87)
¾ cup seedless raspberry jam

INSTRUCTIONS:

1. Prepare dough for almond sandies as directed. Cut cookies into ⅛-inch-thick rounds and reduce baking time to 13 to 15 minutes. Cool cookies completely. (Cookies can be stored in an airtight container for up to 2 days.)

2. Following figures 23 and 24, fill cookies with jam. Serve within 2 hours.

❧

Jam Sandwich Cookies

➤ N O T E : *We especially like raspberry jam because it is free of lumps. Other jams, including apricot, peach, or strawberry, can be used as well. If necessary, push the jam through a mesh strainer to remove any chunks. Chocolate makes an excellent filling for vanilla cookies as well. See the variation below. Makes about 30 sandwich cookies.*

1   recipe Vanilla Icebox Cookies (page 79)
1   cup smooth jam or preserves

▌▌ I N S T R U C T I O N S :

1. Prepare dough for vanilla icebox cookies as directed. Cut dough into ⅛-inch-thick rounds and reduce baking time by a minute or two. Cool cookies completely. (Cookies can be stored in an airtight container for up to 2 days.)

2. Following figures 23 and 24 on page 92, fill cookies with jam. Serve within 2 hours.

▌▌ V A R I A T I O N :

Vanilla Sandwich Cookies with Mocha Filling
A chocolate filling flavored with a little espresso powder is delicious when sandwiched between plain vanilla cookies. If you prefer, omit the espresso powder and use a plain chocolate filling.

Follow recipe for Jam Sandwich Cookies, replacing jam with following filling: Bring ½ cup heavy cream and 1½ teaspoons instant espresso powder to simmer in small saucepan. Turn off heat and add 12 ounces chopped bittersweet or semisweet chocolate. Wait 3 minutes, then whisk until smooth. Let mixture cool to room temperature, at least 30 minutes.

index